FLOORPLAN LAYOUT KIT

The complete room and furniture design set to plan your home, office and garden

1 SQUARE = 1 SQUARE FOOT

SIMPLY DRAW YOUR ROOM SHAPE ON THE GRAPH PAPER, THEN CUT OUT AND POSITION THE FURNITURE!

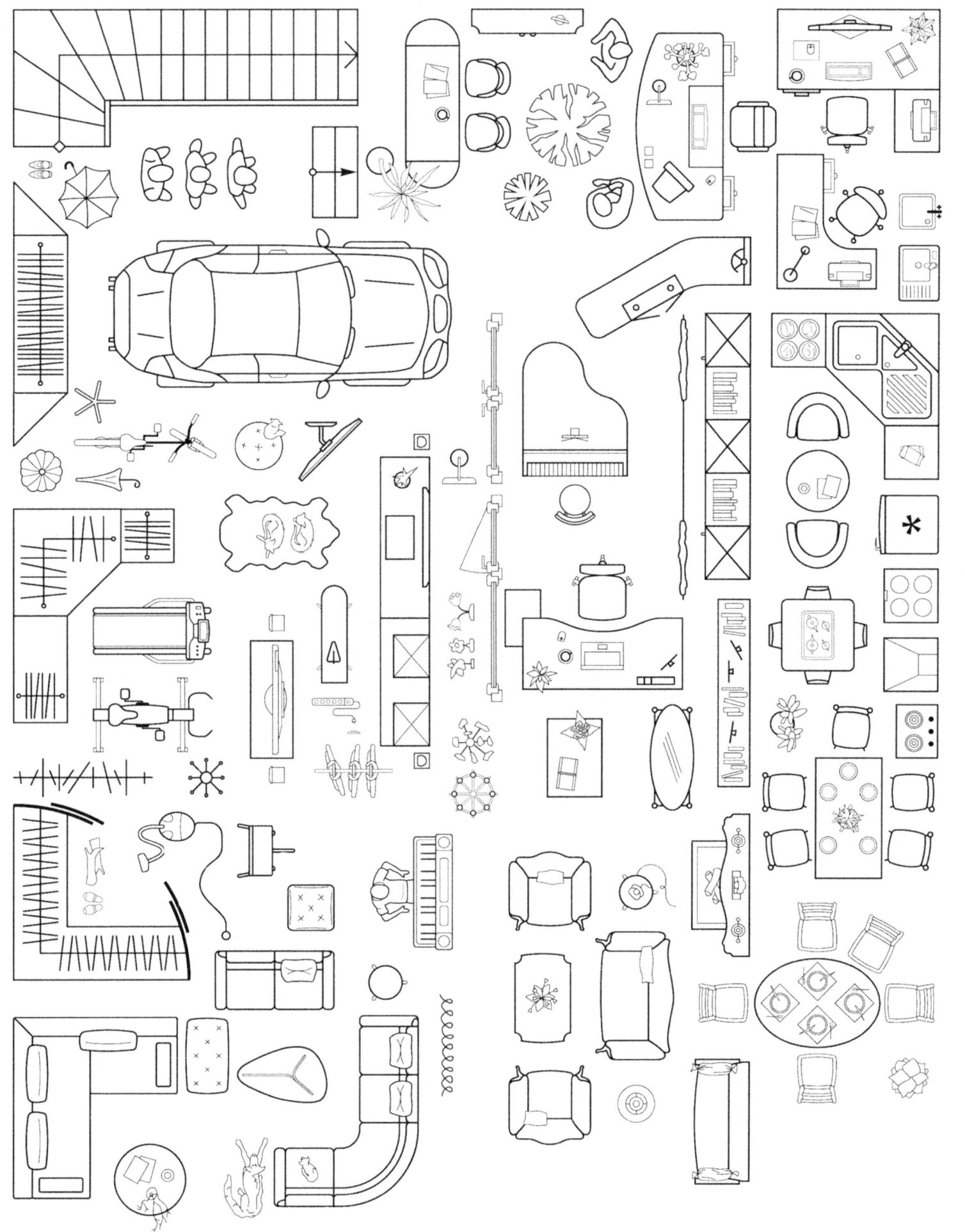

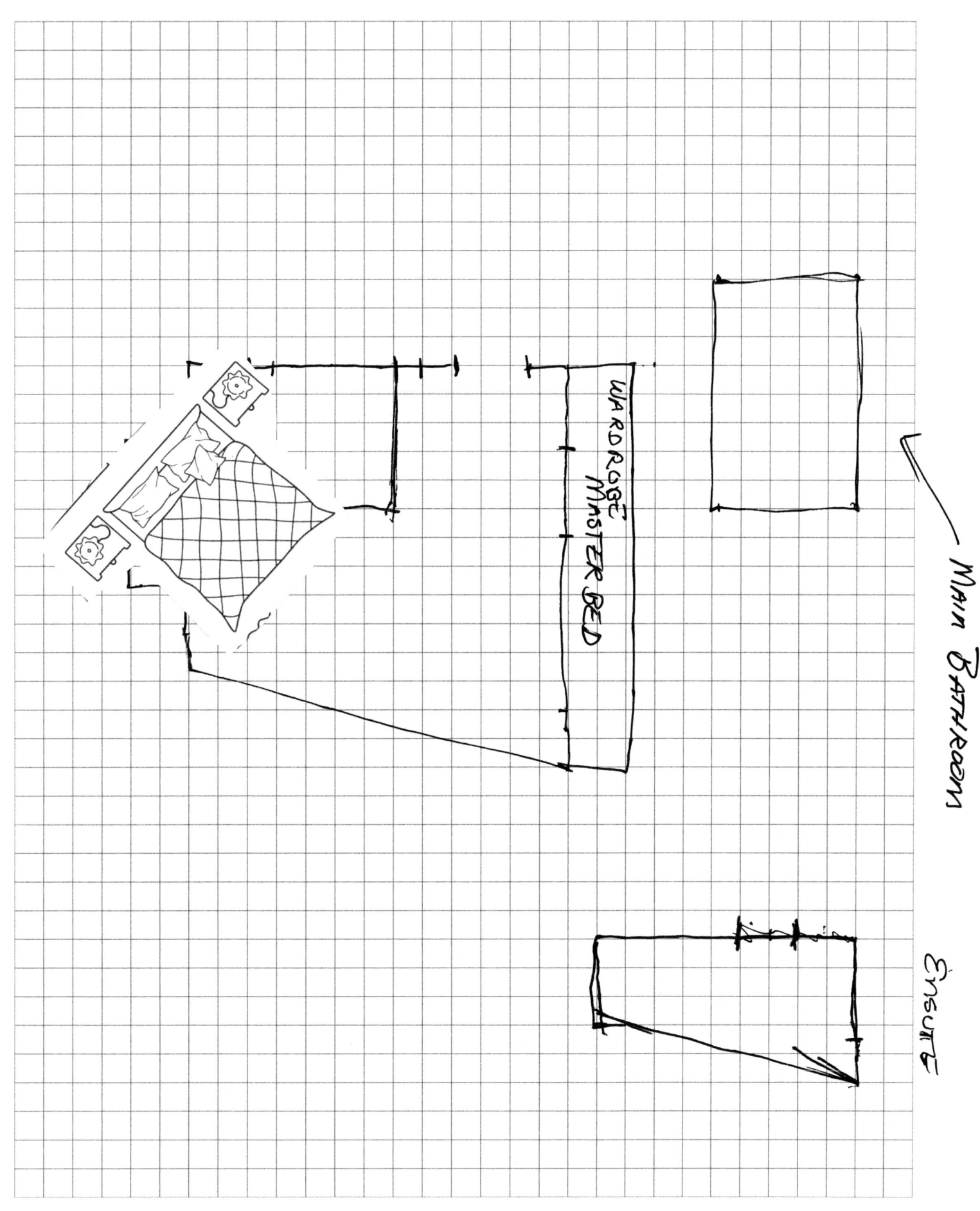

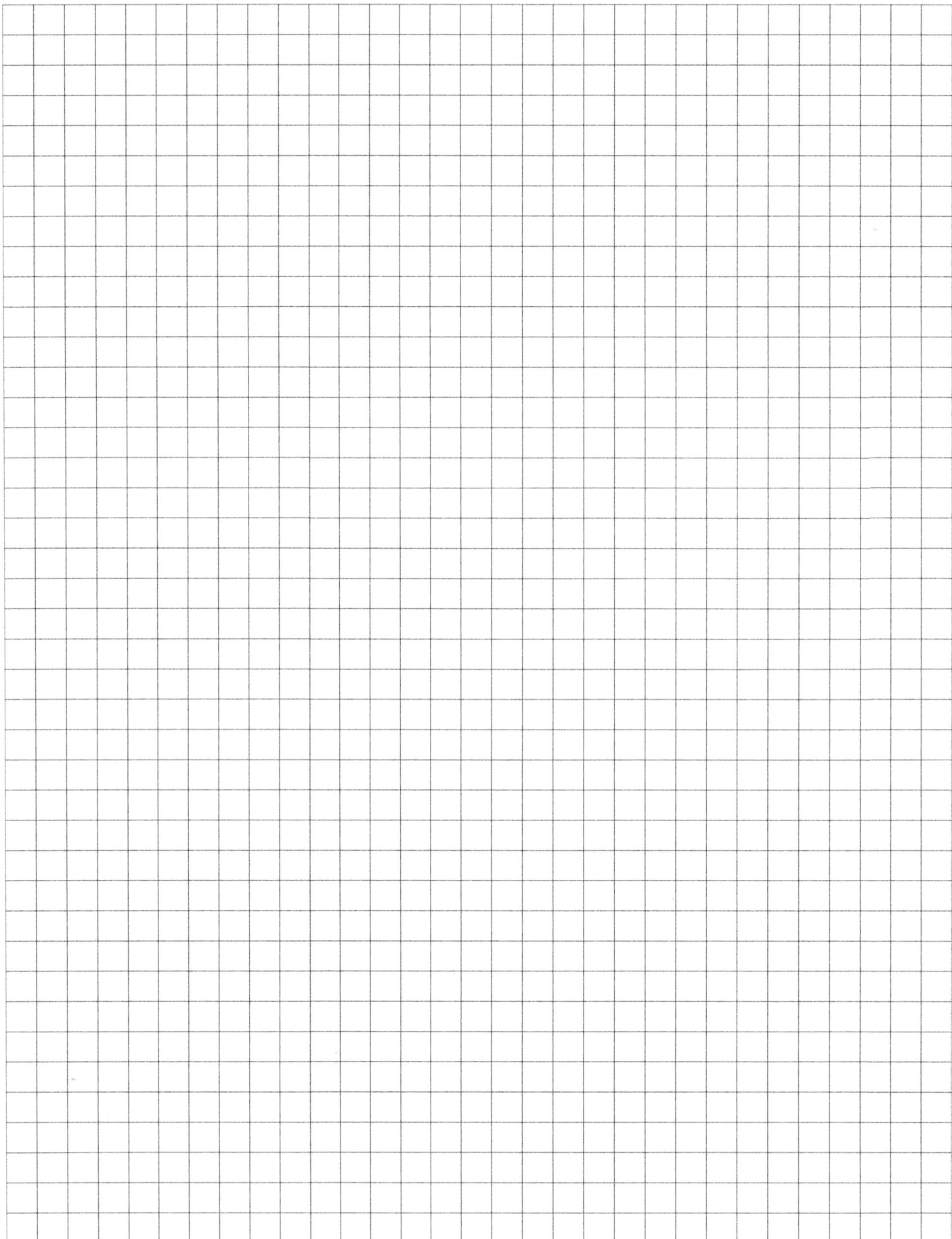

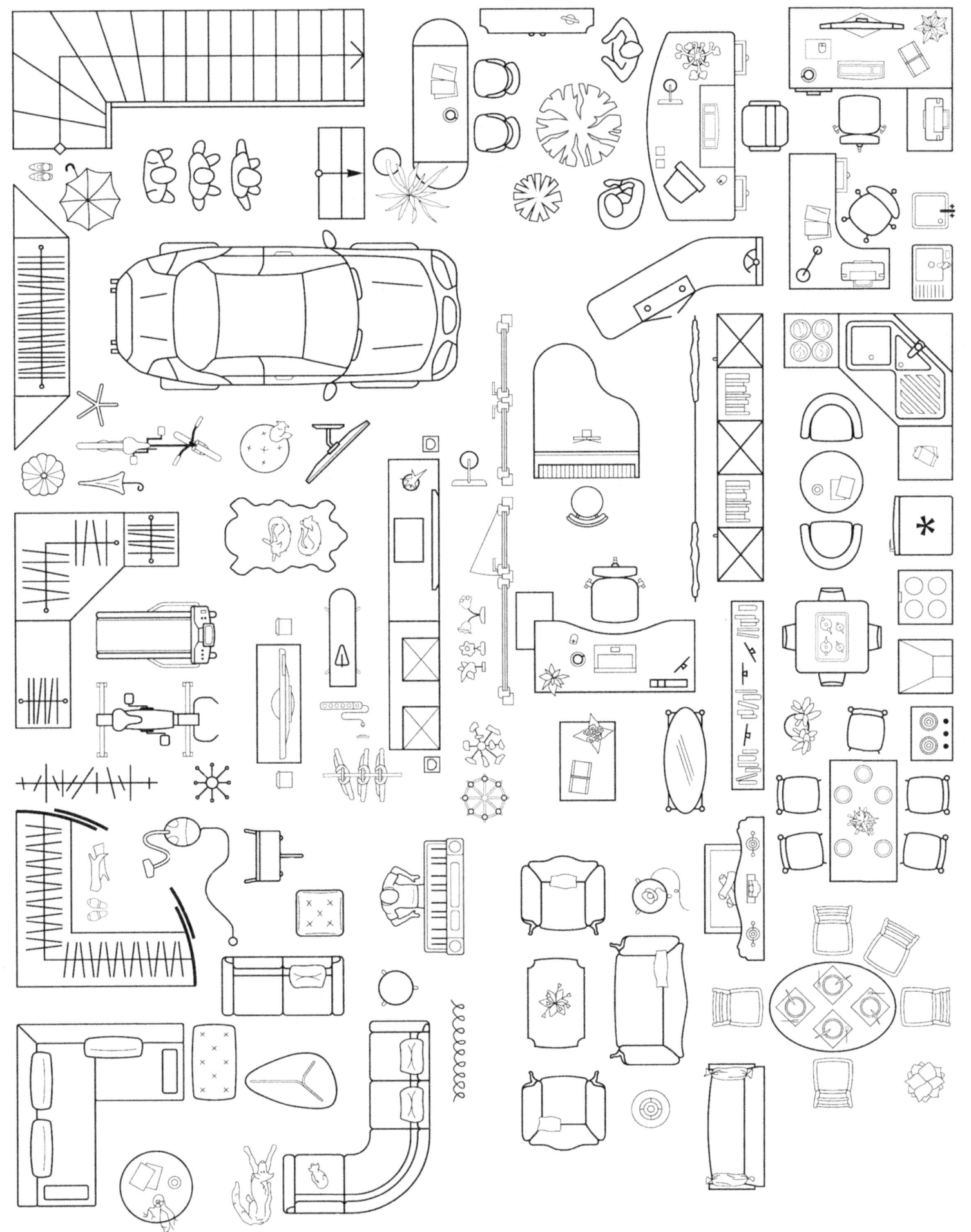

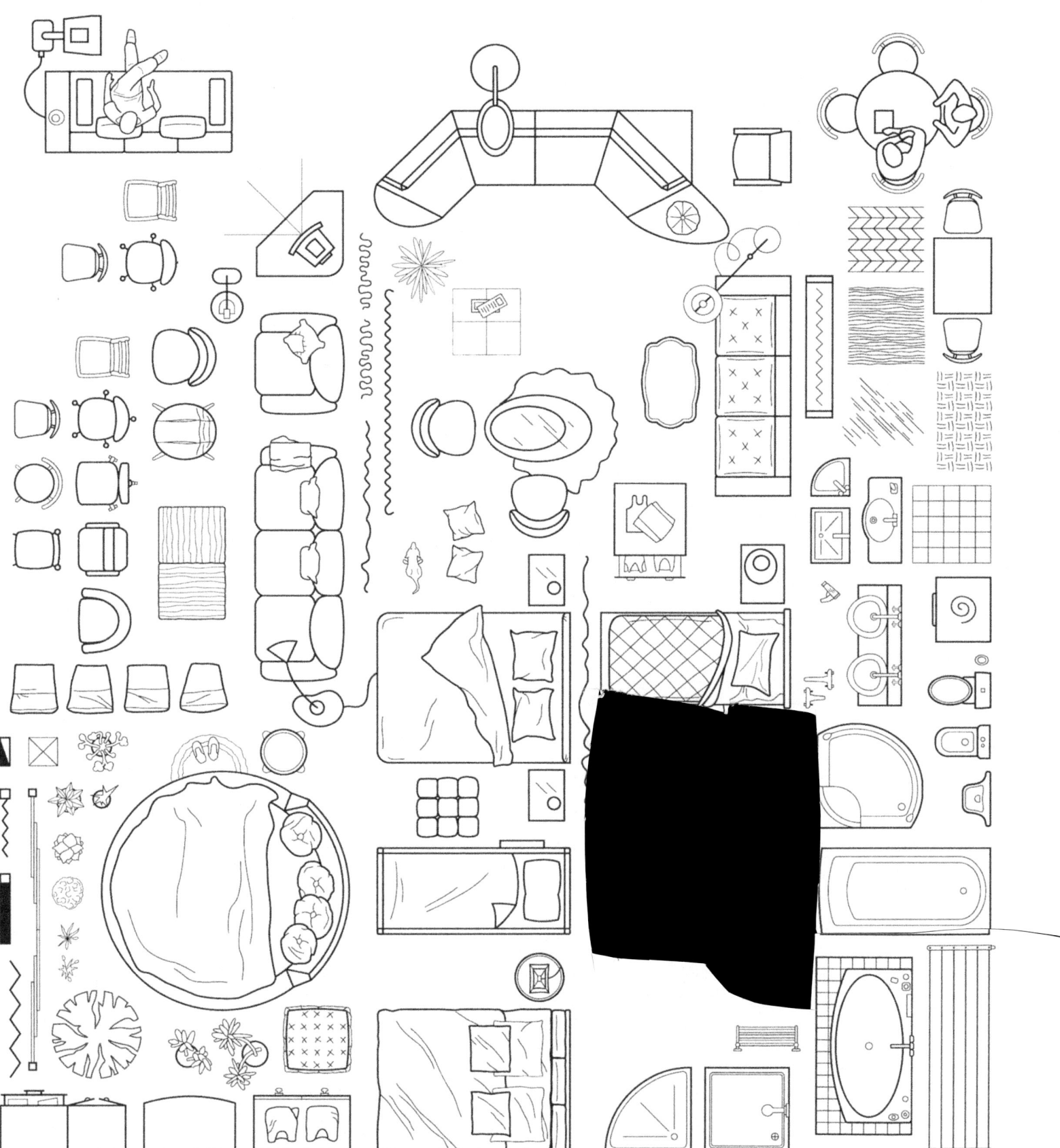

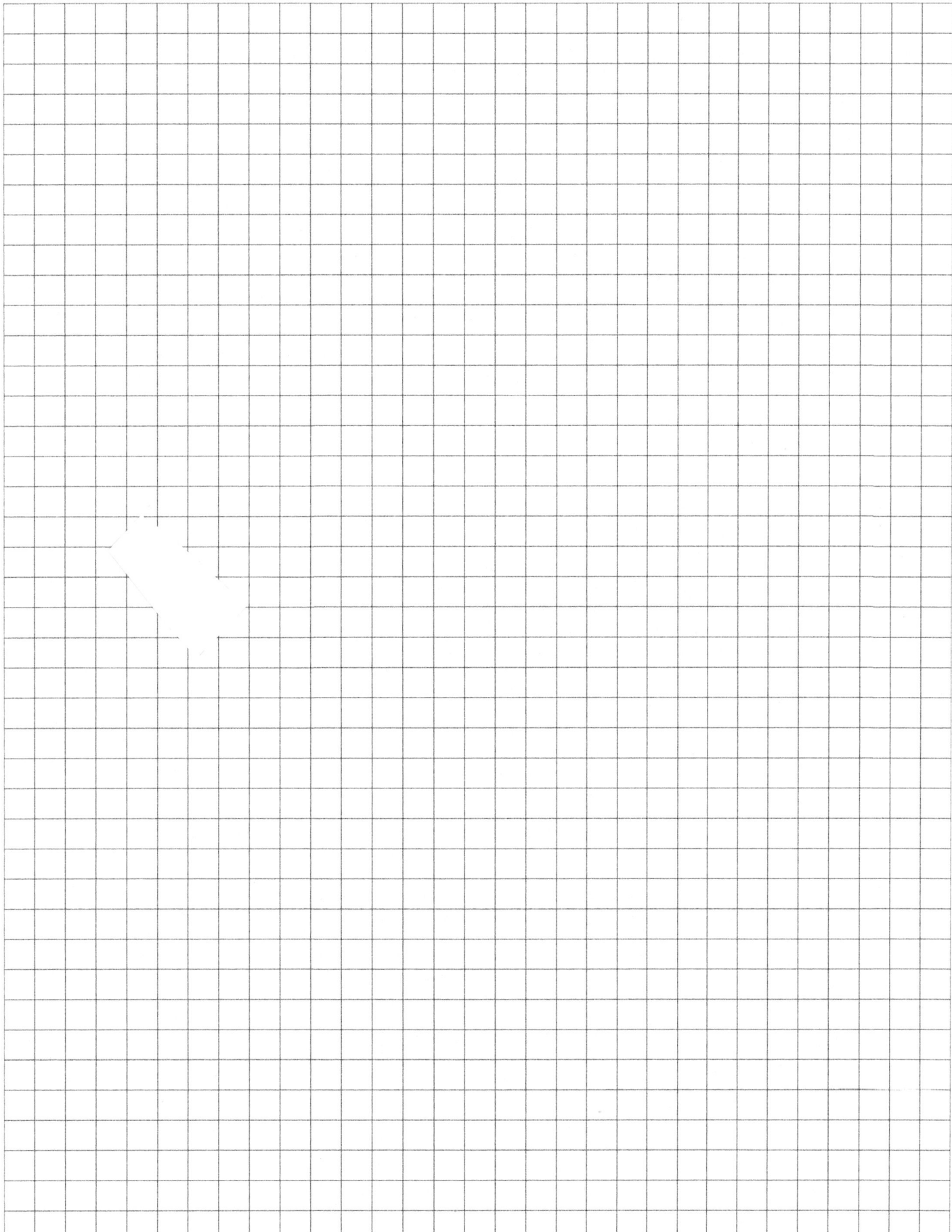

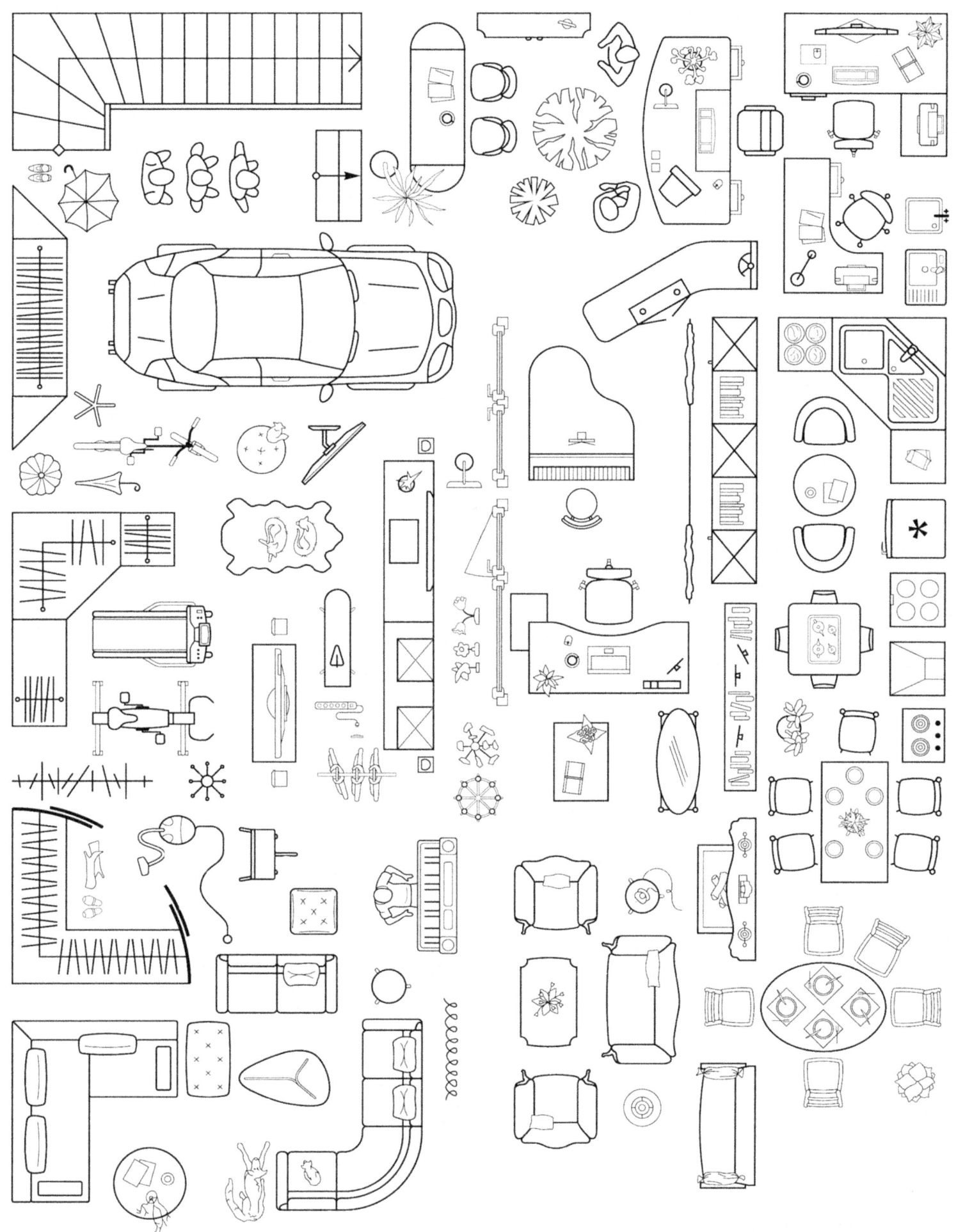

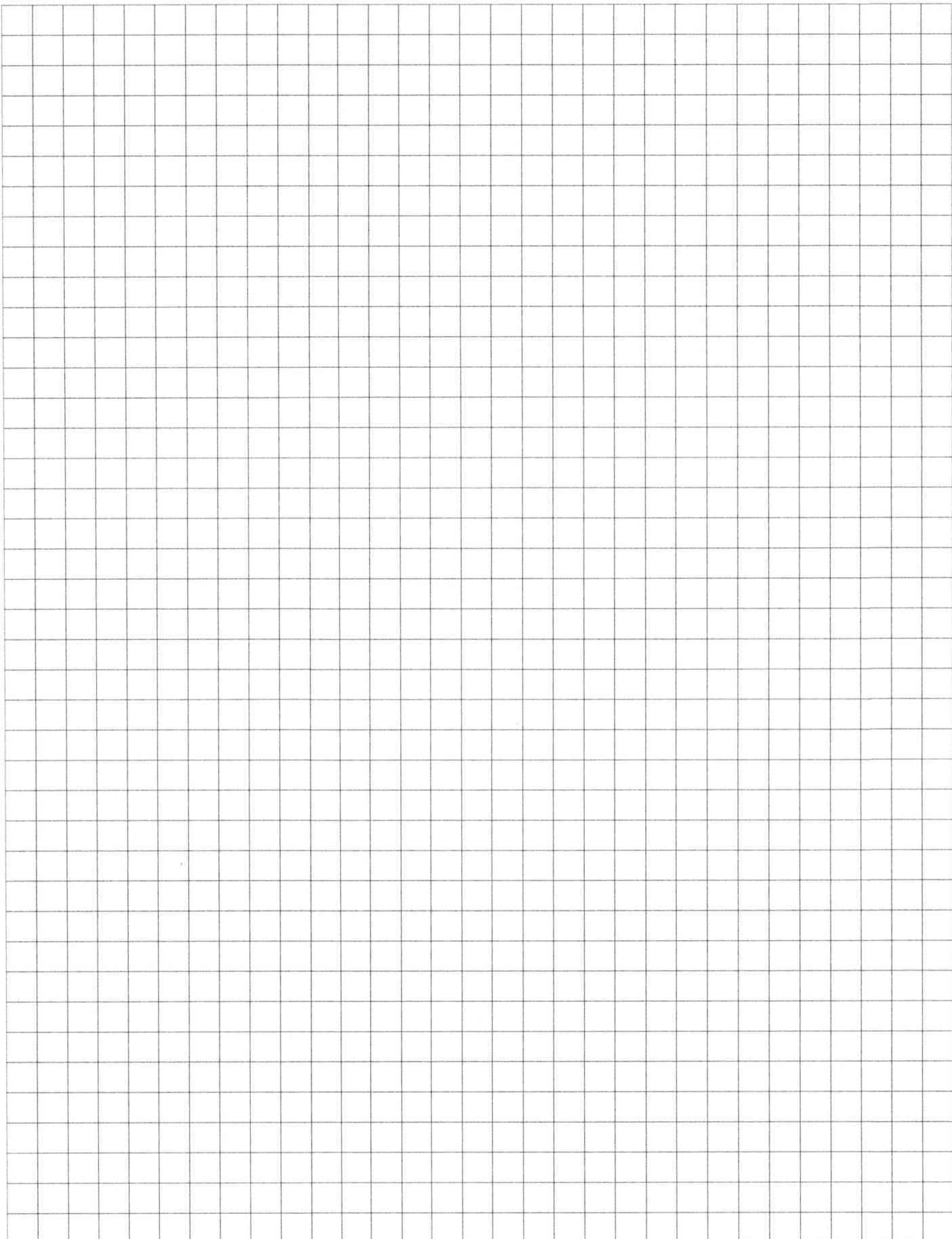

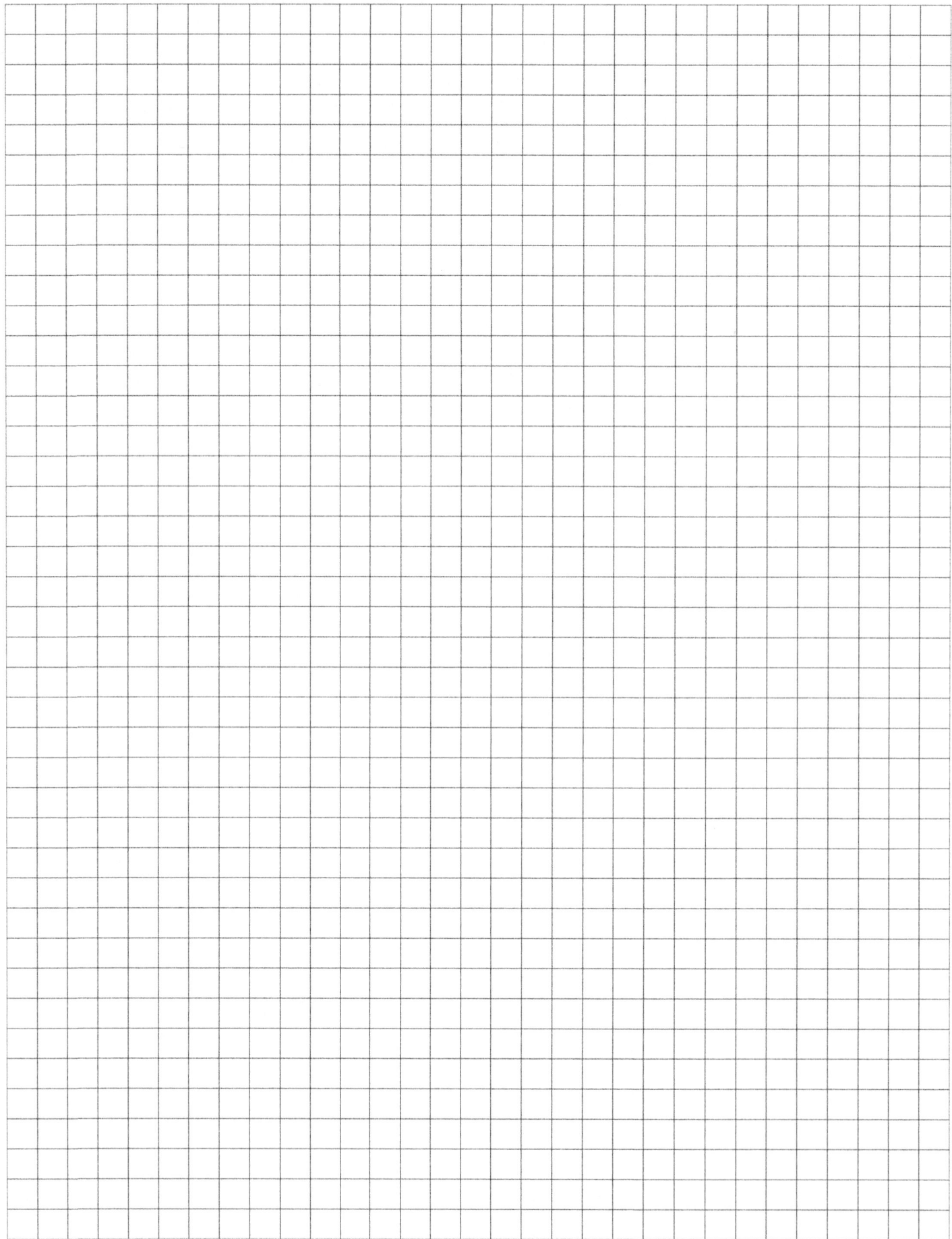

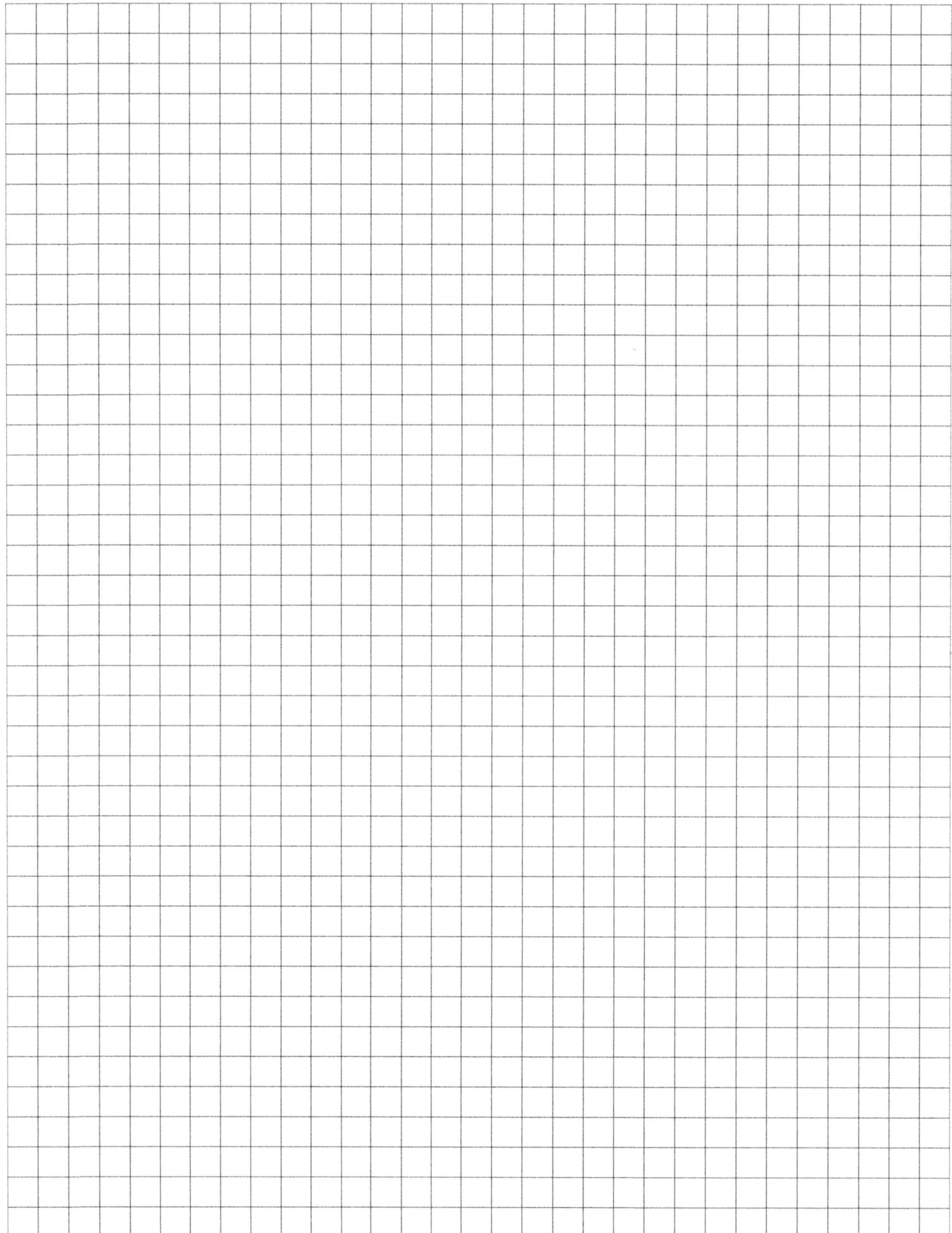

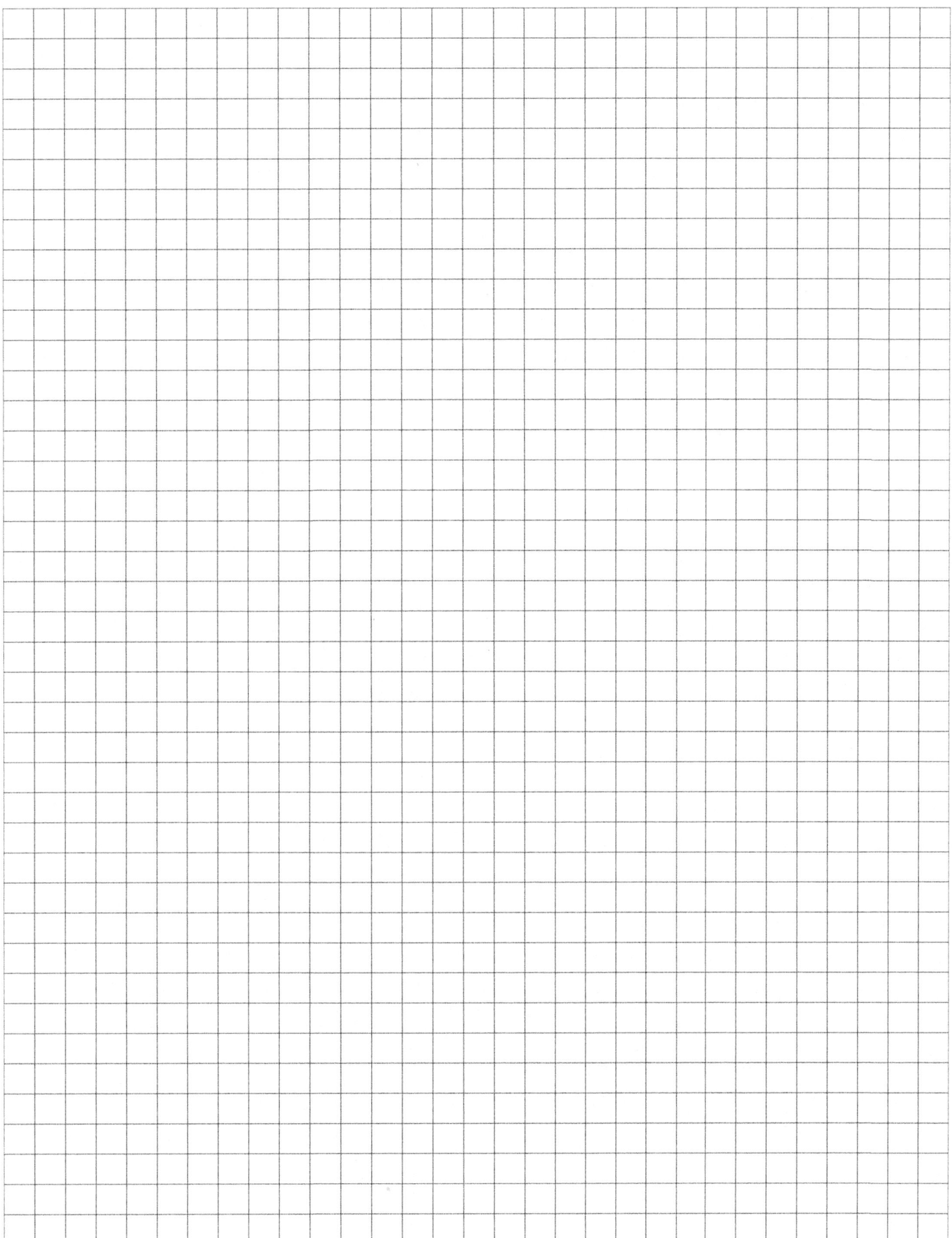

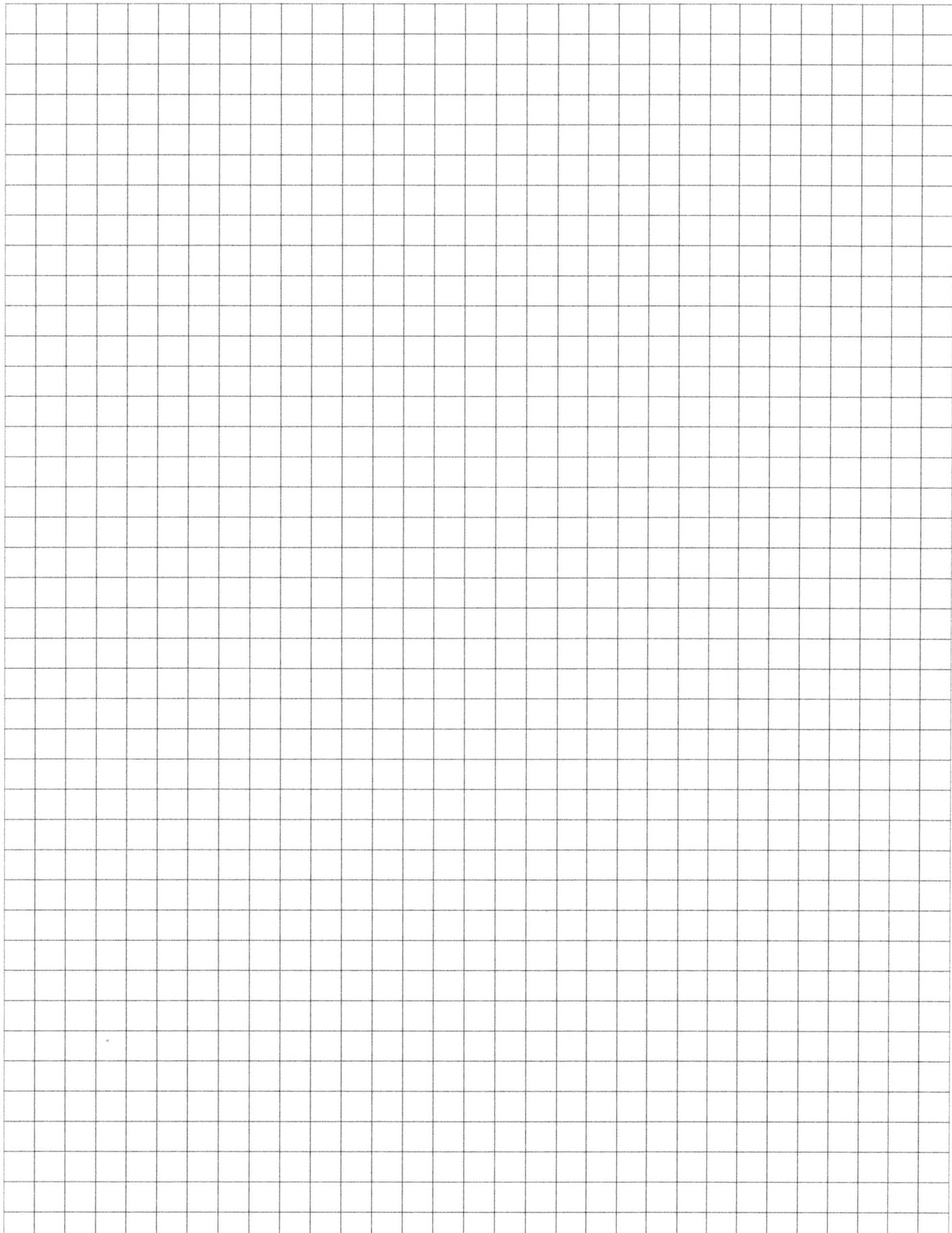

Printed in Dunstable, United Kingdom